The Library of
Big Band Hits

A timeless collection of the greatest hits of the Twenties, Thirties, and Forties when the big band sound held sway over all of popular music. Includes the stories of the bands, their leaders and their singers as well as numerous rare photos. Arranged for piano/vocal with chord names and complete lyrics.

Amsco Publications
New York • London • Sydney

Compiled and edited by Ronny S. Schiff
Editorial design by Elyse Morris Wyman

This book Copyright © 1995 by Amsco Publications,
A Division of Music Sales Corporation, New York

Order No. AM 92126
US International Standard Book Number: 0.8256.1412.0
UK International Standard Book Number: 0.7119.4338.9

Exclusive Distributors:
Music Sales Corporation
257 Park Avenue South, New York, NY 10010 USA
Music Sales Limited
8/9 Frith Street, London W1V 5TZ, England
Music Sales Pty. Limited
120 Rothschild Avenue, Rosebery, Sydney, NSW 2018, Australia

Printed in the United States of America by
Vicks Lithograph and Printing Corporation

CONTENTS

CONTENTS BY BIG BAND

INTRODUCTION

The Big Band Era took root in the Depression and blossomed during the War years. The musicians of these difficult times essentially lived on the road, yet bands managed to find stability despite their transient lifestyles. Members of the groups became family to each other, forming a firm mutual support network. Jo Stafford, one of the great big-band singers, summed up the experience: "Music was no decision for me. It was just always traveling on the road, but what do you know? You're so young…I thought it was fun. Musicians were fun. They have the best sense of humor. They're kind, gentle men; we lived like a family, laughed constantly…I learned a lot from Tommy [Dorsey], a great teacher, and from all the musicians. I was surrounded by some of the best in the world."

The jazz of the twenties served as the seed that ultimately grew into big-band music. Small jazz groups that played in the Dixieland tradition with piano, bass, drums, clarinet, sax or trumpet, and trombone added the blues and improvisational idioms to their sound and more instruments to their ensembles. Although musicians traditionally strove to achieve a kind of "musical ESP"—that supreme chemistry that develops from playing together in a group—they found particular delight in "jamming" with other musicians and getting their "takes" on a solo. Bands gradually grew in size, offering far more musical flexibility and variation. Because larger groups were not as conducive to collective improvisation, bands were forced to play from arrangements, or "charts," which featured solos by lead musicians at specific points. Hence the addition of an essential new "player": the big-band arranger.

There were several individuals in particular who significantly contributed to the rise of the big bands: Ben Pollack's bands in the late twenties and early thirties included musical wizards Charlie Spivak, Jimmy McPartland, Bud Freeman, Gil Rodin, Benny Goodman, Glenn Miller, and later, Harry James. Pollack, with an unrivaled ear and the uncanny ability to recognize superior talent, was the primary catalyst for the Big Band Era. Record industry kings also made notable contributions to the music. Eli Oberstein, who served as Victor's A&R chief, and producer John Hammond at Columbia were each responsible for nurturing the careers of many very famous artists. Booking agents Willard Alexander and Si Shribman; managers such as Irving Mills, Cork O'Keefe, and Joe Glaser; radio DJs Al Jarvis and Martin Block; and critic/big-band historian George Simon also influenced the careers of many of this era's musical greats.

*Consummate manager
Joe Glaser*

The bandleaders of the big bands displayed amazing musical versatility. Most of them had extensive classical-music backgrounds and were conservatory or university trained. Many of them "doubled"—that is, played more than one instrument—as well as leading the group. Even some of the singers doubled as instrumentalists. Though we refer to the groups these days as 'big bands,' one should take note that the prominent aggregations were known as 'orchestras' by contemporaries due to the fact that they included string sections.

Radio was a particularly popular form of entertainment during the Big Band Era, spanning the generation gap and appealing to the entire family. True, there were the "bobby-soxers"— the teens of the forties who swooned over Sinatra, Eberly, or Monroe—but young and old enjoyed gathering around the radio set to listen to a big-band broadcast.

Many elements contributed to a band's popularity. Besides the amount of radio play a band received, an obviously weighty factor, the actual location of the radio broadcast often had significant influence over which bands were successful. Big-city broadcasts from places like the Glen Island Casino in New Rochelle, New York City's Roseland Ballroom and the Cotton Club, and Hollywood's Palladium gave radio listeners a glimpse of the big hot spots of the times as well as drawing large live audiences. The most popular groups were generally the most "dance-able," with sounds ranging from sweet to swing to true jazz.

Where did the Big Band Era go? It ended with the resolution of World War II. Although the era reached its height during the War years, the War literally bled the bands of their personnel. Groups fell apart because their leaders or key players were drafted or volunteered, and few bands were able to re-form afterward. Those bands that did successfully regroup generally survived by adapting their styles to new tastes, playing nightclubs rather than ballrooms, and hooking in to the new medium—television.

Other factors also hastened the demise of big-band music. The American Society of Composers, Authors and Publishers (ASCAP), whose function was to protect composers' interests, wanted more money from the radio networks when its contract was due for renewal in 1939. Broadcasters set up a rival performance rights society, Broadcast Music, Inc. (BMI), in protest, and in the first ten months of 1941 banned all ASCAP music from the air. BMI, which had a far more liberal membership policy, built up the burgeoning country/western and R&B markets (then known as "hillbilly" and "race" music), and gained a significant piece of the pop market. Even so, many of the big-band composers remained with ASCAP, so there was some lag time before bands found other material or arrangements of public domain songs.

Musical wizard Charlie Spivak

James C. Petrillo, head of the American Federation of Musicians (A.F. of M.), called a strike in August of 1942 demanding payment from the recording companies to offset monies lost from jukeboxes and radio performances, for which musicians received no compensation. Some record companies settled immediately, a few new ones sprang up, and the giants held out until 1944 leaving a big gap in big-band recording history. A small portion of big-band music was saved via V-Disc programs—special recordings the musicians and leaders made voluntarily (and unpaid) for the Armed Forces, and fortunately, some very good sides were cut for this program.

The big bands also produced incidental progress in the breaking down of racial barriers. White musicians in the twenties adopted jazz, which was derived from African-American musical traditions, and shaped it into a popular commercial music. Jazz's popularity resulted in bandleaders' becoming more concerned with the skill of the musician than with the color of his or her skin. Throughout the thirties and forties, policies of segregation were still common in many parts of the country. Ironically, black musicians often found themselves playing in hotels or rooms where they would not have been allowed to attend as part of the audience.

The big bands, their leaders, players, and singers generally enjoyed a free-spirited, unstructured existence. Featured players became leaders, leaders went back to being players, bands broke up and new ones formed combining players from different groups. Players became arrangers, arrangers became leaders, and what is most important, many musicians became songwriters. Perhaps the big-band greats who did manage to survive beyond the early fifties—such as Duke Ellington, Count Basie, Stan Kenton, and Lawrence Welk—did so partly because of their flexibility and stylistic diversity.

Paul Whiteman And His Orchestra

"MOONLIGHT ON THE GANGES" 1926
Austin Young
"MUDDY WATER" 1927
Bing Crosby
"ALL OF ME" 1932
Mildred Bailey
"THREE ON A MATCH" 1932
Red McKenzie

The distinctive face of Paul Whiteman

The words 'mentor' and 'guiding light' are the ones to best fit **Paul Whiteman**. He was dubbed the King of Jazz in the twenties, though it was his featured soloists (the Dorseys, the Teagardens, Bix Beiderbecke, Joe Venuti, Frank Trumbauer, Bunny Berigan, Eddie Lang, Johnny Mercer), not necessarily his own band's arrangements, who were responsible for the words 'jazz' and 'Whiteman' becoming synonymous.

Classically trained Whiteman (he had played in the Denver Symphony Orchestra) was a fabulous showman and a good person. The latter trait he no doubt inherited from his father, the Director of Music Education for the Denver City Schools, who was known for the support and encouragement he gave to legions of Colorado musicians. He respected and admired the musicians with whom he worked, paid them handsomely, and was always encouraging and nurturing new artists. One of his earliest arrangers was Ferde Grofé, who orchestrated the original version of George Gershwin's "Rhapsody in Blue" for its premier by the Whiteman band.

Singer Mildred Bailey

Mildred Bailey had the classic beginnings of a kid of her era—she plugged songs at the music counter of a five-and-dime store in Spokane, and later moved on to jobs at local clubs. In 1925, she moved to Los Angeles where she wowed Angelenos at various speakeasies and married a bootlegger. Her brother Al Rinker and his sidekick **Bing Crosby** drove to Los Angeles to see her perform and decided to stay when she got them a singing job.

Paul Whiteman heard Crosby and Rinker at the Metropolitan Theater in Los Angeles and liked what he heard. By this time he was at the top of his field, and he polished the duo's act for his very sophisticated audiences by teaming them with Harry Barris and dubbing the trio the Rhythm Boys. The audiences loved Crosby, although he was a handful for Whiteman, being somewhat of a troublemaker. Crosby benefited from working with fine jazzmen like trumpeter Bix Beiderbecke and singer Red McKenzie ("Three on a Match"). In 1927, Crosby cut his first solo recording, "Muddy Water," with Whiteman's group and made it to the charts. He also appeared in the landmark film *The King of Jazz* with Whiteman in 1930 before striking out on his own.

Singer Bing Crosby

Al Rinker invited Whiteman to a party at Mildred Bailey's Hollywood Hills house. When Whiteman heard her sing "Sleepy Time Gal," he hired her immediately to sing on his radio show. She was Whiteman's first female band singer, and may have been the first woman to sing solo with any big band. Crosby credited her with influencing his style. When she sang, she had clarity, wonderful enunciation, fine phrasing, fabulous intonation, and a pretty sound—an effortless sound. With this fine instrument, she was able to record a wide variety of material. She was a tremendous influence on other female singers of the era.

MOONLIGHT ON THE GANGES

Words by Chester Wallace, Music by Sherman Myers

MUDDY WATER

Words by Jo Trent, Music by Peter De Rose and Harry Richmond

15

ALL OF ME

Words & Music by Seymour Simons and Gerald Marks

one-sid-ed love __ af-fair? All you took, I

glad-ly gave. There's noth-ing left for me to save.

Chorus:

All of me, _____ Why not take all of me, _____

Can't you see _____ I'm no good with-

THREE ON A MATCH

Words by Raymond B. Egan, Music by Ted Fio Rito

Nat Shilkret And The Victor Orchestra
"HALLELUJAH!" 1927
Franklyn Baur

An alumnus of Sousa's band, clarinetist **Nat Shilkret** also played in the New York Philharmonic before taking the baton as Victor Records' Director of Light Music (i.e., Pop); a position that he held for thirty years! His studio orchestra not only backed up many of Victor's artists, they also made a multitude of recordings, often covering current Broadway show tunes or motion picture themes. Their 1927 version of "Hallelujah!" was from the Broadway musical *Hit the Deck*.

Tenor **Franklyn Baur** had been part of the twenties' most popular singing group, the Revelers, who also recorded "Hallelujah!" in 1927.

Rudy Vallee And His Connecticut Yankees
"(I'M IN LOVE WITH YOU) HONEY" 1929
Rudy Vallee

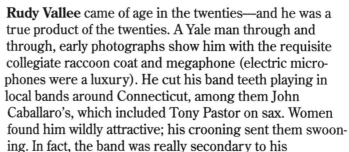

Rudy Vallee with megaphone
(photo courtesy of Ian Whitcomb)

Rudy Vallee

(courtesy of Ian Whitcomb)

Rudy Vallee came of age in the twenties—and he was a true product of the twenties. A Yale man through and through, early photographs show him with the requisite collegiate raccoon coat and megaphone (electric microphones were a luxury). He cut his band teeth playing in local bands around Connecticut, among them John Caballaro's, which included Tony Pastor on sax. Women found him wildly attractive; his crooning sent them swooning. In fact, the band was really secondary to his singing, and his romantic style truly set a sound for crooners to copy well into the thirties. "Honey," introduced on his radio program in 1929, sold a million copies of sheet music in only one year! Vallee continuously charted in the Top 20 from 1929 to 1946.

Guy Lombardo And His Royal Canadians
"SWEETHEARTS ON PARADE" 1929
"HEARTACHES" 1931
Carmen Lombardo

Billed as the "sweetest music this side of heaven," **Guy Lomabardo**'s band was a romantic band—anyone could dance to it, romance to it. He set a certain warm mood and chose lovely melodic tunes; his style was unmistakable. Three brothers—leader Guy, saxist and singer **Carmen**, and trumpeter Lebert—formed the band in the early twenties in London, Ontario, moving throughout the big-band venues until they reached the Roosevelt Grill in New York City. Guy was known as an extraordinarily nice man and a fine businessman. The band personnel stayed the same for years and they enjoyed hit after hit on the *Billboard* charts from 1929 to 1954, selling over 100 million records—more than any other big band. Amazingly, critics report that the joy, enthusiasm, and pride of musicianship always showed through. It was Lombardo's band that was called on for every manner of major occasions, especially Presidential inaugural balls. Of course, Lombardo will be remembered as each year closes: it's his rendition of "Auld Lang Syne" that is always played.

Guy Lombardo

(I'M IN LOVE WITH YOU) HONEY

Words & Music by Seymour Simons, Haven Gillespie and Richard A. Whiting

28

HALLELUJAH!

Words by Leo Robin and Clifford Gray, Music by Vincent Youmans

Moderately, with spirit (in 2)

I'm re - call - in' times when I was small, in light and free jub - i - lee days.

shoo the _____ blues a - way. _____ When cares pur -

sue ya, _____ "Hal - le - lu - jah," ____ Gets you

through the _____ dark - est day. _____

Sa - tan _____ lies a - wait - in' _____ and cre -

HEARTACHES

Words & Music by Al Hoffman and John Kilmer

SWEETHEARTS ON PARADE

Words & Music by Carmen Lombardo and Charles Newman

And as they pass they make me feel so blue;
I won-der if my dreams will e'er come true;

CHORUS *Not fast*

Two by two, _____ They go march-ing thru, _____ the

SWEET-HEARTS ON PA - RADE, _____ I can't help cry,

As they pass me by, _____ the SWEET-HEARTS ON PA -

Ted Fio Rito And His Orchestra
"(WHEN IT'S) DARKNESS ON THE DELTA" 1933
Muzzy Marcellino

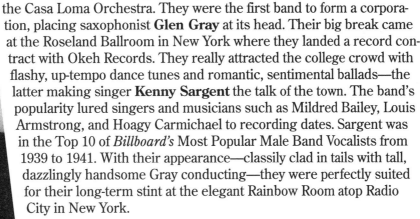

Ted Fio Rito

Ted Fio Rito's long-term claim to fame would have to be the pop songs he wrote that became standards: "Charley, My Boy," "I Never Knew," "Laugh, Clown Laugh." He set up his first band in the twenties, and by the thirties had established a sweet-sounding group with some gimmicks (novelty instruments like temple blocks and Hammond organ and a tricky singing bass player).

The band's singer was **Muzzy Marcellino**, a pleasant-voiced man who was later known for his whistling on the soundtrack to the film *The High and the Mighty*. The band also had a famous singer for a short time: Betty Grable.

Glen Gray And The Casa Loma Orchestra
"IT'S THE TALK OF THE TOWN" 1933
"UNDER A BLANKET OF BLUE" 1933
Kenny Sargent

The very dapper Glen Gray

In 1929, a group of Detroit musicians were scheduled to open a new Canadian nightclub, the Casa Loma. The club never opened, but the group stayed together and retained the name of the Casa Loma Orchestra. They were the first band to form a corporation, placing saxophonist **Glen Gray** at its head. Their big break came at the Roseland Ballroom in New York where they landed a record contract with Okeh Records. They really attracted the college crowd with flashy, up-tempo dance tunes and romantic, sentimental ballads—the latter making singer **Kenny Sargent** the talk of the town. The band's popularity lured singers and musicians such as Mildred Bailey, Louis Armstrong, and Hoagy Carmichael to recording dates. Sargent was in the Top 10 of *Billboard's* Most Popular Male Band Vocalists from 1939 to 1941. With their appearance—classily clad in tails with tall, dazzlingly handsome Gray conducting—they were perfectly suited for their long-term stint at the elegant Rainbow Room atop Radio City in New York.

Ben Bernie And His Orchestra
"LET'S ALL SING LIKE THE BIRDIES SING" 1933
Pat Kennedy

Ben Bernie was known as "The Ol' Maestro," since he had been fronting bands as early as in the twenties. His signature "Yow-sah" and his warm, half-singing-half-talking delivery endeared him to his fans, and his musicians adored him. His recording of "Let's All Sing Like the Birdies Sing" is ample evidence of his flair for the comedic. His band's popularity was helped along in no small measure by the location of their home base: they enjoyed a long stay at the Pabst Blue Ribbon Casino at the Chicago World's Fair.

Pat Kennedy was one of the many fine vocalists in Bernie's stable—which also included, for a very short time, a young Dinah Shore fresh from Nashville, Tennessee.

LET'S ALL SING LIKE THE BIRDIES SING

Words by Robert Hargreaves, Stanley Damerell, Music by Tolchard Evans

But when the dick - y birds sing in the trees,
Let's all the roost in the trees, or else in - stead.

I feel we ought to try and sing like these.
In your ca - nar - y's cage make up a bed.

chorus
Let's all sing like the bird - ies sing,

43

(WHEN IT'S)
DARKNESS ON THE DELTA

Words by Marty Symes and Al Neiburg, Music by Jerry Livingston

IT'S THE TALK OF THE TOWN

Words by Marty Symes and Al Neiburg, Music by Jerry Livingston

It's the talk of the town. town.

Instrumental solo

We

UNDER A BLANKET OF BLUE

Words & Music by Al Neiburg, Marty Symes and Jerry Livingston

Benny Goodman And His [Swing] Orchestra

"DARN THAT DREAM" 1940
Mildred Bailey
"JERSEY BOUNCE" 1942 • "WE'LL MEET AGAIN" 1942
Peggy Lee

Benny Goodman was a prodigy. By age sixteen, he was playing clarinet with
Art Kassel. Like many of the jazz-oriented musicians described herein, he cut his
musical teeth in Ben Pollack's band. Goodman was with the Pollack band from 1925 to
'29, then did studio work and formed his own band in 1934 (although he was on the
charts as early as 1931). His radio break came in 1935 when he was scheduled every
Saturday night to play for a three-hour marathon dance-band program along with
Xavier Cugat's and Ken Murray's bands. Goodman's jazz/swing sound initially didn't
make it with some unsophisticated ears, but his booking agent, Willard Alexander, and
producer *extraordinaire* John Hammond were both behind him all the way. After many
one-niters, they were booked into Los Angeles's premiere night spot, the Palomar
Ballroom, where they tore down the house. When they moved east to Chicago's
Congress Hotel, Goodman was dubbed the "King of Swing." He was the one who
brought the big-band sound and jazz together to form swing, hard-driving swing at that.
George Simon, the number-one big-band chronicler and historian, credits Goodman as
the one who "started the big-band craze."

Benny Goodman—The King of Swing

Jack Teagarden, remembered for his trombone stylings, took male-singer duty in
these early days. Helen Ward also sang with Goodman during this period. Her style as
a jazz singer and pianist with a warm sound was well suited to the style of the Goodman
band. She went on to sing with several other top-flight bands.

By 1936, Goodman's band was winning the jazz magazine polls, and they were back in
Hollywood working on their first movie, *The Big Broadcast of 1937*. In 1938 they performed
their infamous Carnegie Hall concert to a sellout, dancing-in-the-aisles crowd of fans who
were knocked out by the interplay of Gene Krupa's drums and Goodman's clarinet. Star
musicians and arrangers were joining the band and would continue to do so; notably,
arrangers Fletcher Henderson and Eddie Sauter (see Glenn Miller); musicians Jack
Teagarden, Claude Thornhill, Gene Krupa, Bunny Berigan, Ziggy Elman, Harry James,
Charlie Christian, Bud Freeman, Johnny Guarnieri, Cootie Williams, Billy Butterfield, Kai
Winding, Stan Getz, Zoot Sims, and Mel Powell. There was also a fascinating array of
singers including Martha Tilton, **Mildred Bailey**, Helen Forrest, Buddy Greco, and
Johnny Mercer. Goodman was unique in that he often broke up the band into smaller units
and invited guest soloists to play on his records. Notable instances include his recordings
with Teddy Wilson, Lionel Hampton, and Ella Fitzgerald.

Singer Mildred Bailey

Various musicians, such as Krupa and James, came and went throughout the late
thirties, changing the texture of the band. The 1941 lineup of musicians was spectacularly
solid and was augmented by the addition of jazz singer **Peggy Lee**. She'd sung briefly with
crooning bandleader Will Osborne; Goodman first heard her in a Chicago cocktail lounge.
Lee was a team player, understanding the importance of musical interplay with the musicians. Much was made of Lee's ability to phrase and improvise, her rhythmic acuity, her
sensual voice, and her budding flair for songwriting that would become evident in years to
come. The Goodman band continued unabated and was wildly popular until 1946.

*Lionel Hampton
with Benny Goodman*

DARN THAT DREAM

Words & Music by Jimmy Van Heusen and Edgar De Lange

Darn that dream____ I dream each night.____
Darn your lips____ and darn your eyes,____

60

JERSEY BOUNCE

Words by Robert Wright,
Music by Bobby Platter, Tiny Bradshaw, Ed Johnson and Robert Wright

put it right on the air _____ And now you hear it ev - 'ry - where ___

Up - town ___ gave it new licks ___ Down - town ___ add-ed some tricks ___ No town ___

makes it sound the same ___ As where it came from! So if you don't feel so hot ___

_____ Go out to some Jer - sey spot. _____ And wheth-er you're hep or not ___

_____ The Jer - sey bounce-'ll make you swing. ___ They

63

WE'LL MEET AGAIN

Words & Music by Ross Parker and Charles Hughes

set you, ___ I'll not for-get you, ___ sweet-heart.
mor-row, ___ Good-bye to sor-row, ___ my dear.

Moderately slow, with expression

Chorus

We'll meet a-gain, Don't know where, don't know

when, But I know we'll meet a-gain some sun-ny

The Dorsey Brothers Orchestra
"TINY LITTLE FINGERPRINTS" 1935
Kay Weber

Brothers **Jimmy Dorsey** and **Tommy Dorsey** played with many of the great bands of the twenties before joining forces in the early thirties to form their various Dorsey Brothers studio bands. These part-time groups earned a solid reputation for their expert backup on recordings by Bing Crosby, the Boswell Sisters, and Mildred Bailey. They also recorded some of their own instrumentals. In 1934, they turned the group into the full-time Dorsey Brothers Orchestra—a swinging, full-sounding group that included Tommy and Glenn Miller on trombones; Jimmy on clarinet, sax, and occasionally trumpet; Charlie Spivak on trumpet; and Ray McKinley on drums and vocals. Miller also took on arranging chores and tapped several excellent musicians from other bands to join the group, including singer **Kay Weber**.

Weber, known for her beautiful ballad delivery, was the Dorsey brothers' only female singer, and she managed to share slots on the charts with a few male counterparts—Bob Crosby (whose group Weber subsequently joined) and Bob Eberly.

The Dorsey Brothers

The band was meticulously well rehearsed and gained instant respect for their hip swing and jazz sound. However, despite their success, the relationship between the brothers was volatile, and during a gig at the prestigious Glen Island Casino, Tommy walked off the bandstand, never to return.

Isham Jones And His Orchestra
"(THERE IS) NO GREATER LOVE" 1936
Woody Herman

There were few groups that had the lush, rich sound of **Isham Jones'** groups. Jones had been recording since the twenties and had turned "Stardust" into a standard, but it was in the mid thirties that he reached his zenith. His sound was enhanced by an ensemble of truly wonderful musicians; notably, Sonny Lee, Pee Wee Erwin, Johnny Carlson, and arranger Gordon Jenkins. Jones was also known for the many standards that he wrote, such as, "I'll See You in My Dreams," "It Had to Be You," and "There Is No Greater Love."

This last song was recorded by a young singer and saxophone player in Jones's 1936 band, **Woody Herman**. Herman was a good singer, especially of ballads, but his fame was made the next year when he fronted a new band made up of Jones alumni (Jones had disbanded his group) and other fine musicians. The band played a lot of blues, with Herman taking swinging clarinet solos, and it took them until 1939 to find a groove that clicked with the public. When they did, the Herd, as the band was called, was wildly successful. Herman was a man with whom everyone loved to work; his musicians obviously enjoyed themselves. He was the consummate leader and manager. He gave generations of musicians, composers, and arrangers their musical breaks.

Woody Herman as a leader

TINY LITTLE FINGERPRINTS

Words by Charles Newman and Charlie Tobias, Music by Sam Stept

(THERE IS) NO GREATER LOVE

Music by Isham Jones, Words by Marty Symes

man - y dif - f'rent kinds of love, it's true.

The stars all love the moon - beams, A -

way up in the blue. But there nev - er was a

love like mine for you._____ There is no

poco rit.

mf

Ozzie Nelson And His Orchestra
"IS IT TRUE WHAT THEY SAY ABOUT DIXIE?" 1936
Ozzie Nelson

Oswald George Nelson was from the Rudy Vallee school of big band: sweet, pleasant, collegiate. He was a graduate of Rutgers University, where they've always had a great music department, and he knew his market. The band's first national break was when they played at the Glen Island Casino in the summer of 1932. The band's rich sound was due to full brass and sax sections and duo pianos. Nelson's singing style was relaxed and musical with a slight jazz tinge. His early singing partner, Harriet Hilliard, was gorgeous and talented. She contributed vocals to a good number of duets in the band's repertoire, but, of course, Ozzie and Harriet shall always be best remembered for their television adventures.

Jimmy Dorsey And His Orchestra
"IS IT TRUE WHAT THEY SAY ABOUT DIXIE?" 1936 • "(I'M AFRAID) THE MASQUERADE IS OVER" 1939 • "BLUE CHAMPAGNE" 1941
Bob Eberly
"SIX LESSONS FROM MADAME LA ZONGA" 1940
Helen O'Connell

Jimmy Dorsey and his Orchestra with Jack Cassidy and Jane Wyman in Hollywood Canteen

Jimmy Dorsey took up the reins of the Dorsey Brothers band, and although Jimmy was of a shy, quiet nature, he was still a great leader. He had extensive experience: he'd enjoyed wide popularity as a sideman on radio gigs and on recordings with the groups he'd put together with his brother Tommy. One of these groups, Dorsey's Wild Canaries, was one of the first jazz groups to broadcast on radio, and the groups and artists he'd played with in the twenties read like a Who's Who of jazz: Jean Goldkette, Vincent Lopez, Paul Whiteman, Red Nichols, Joe Venuti, and Ted Lewis, to name a few. Although Jimmy himself was a consummate jazzer, his band leaned toward more of a danceable pop sound rather than hard jazz, although they recorded many swinging instrumentals. The band stayed on the charts from their beginning in 1935 up to 1950, partially due to their great media exposure from a long radio stretch on Bing Crosby's *Kraft Music Hall* program and their appearance in several movies. The arranging staff was first rate with the likes of Tutti Camarata, Don Redman, and Hal Mooney, and during the forties the band included musicians such as Johnny Guarnieri and Herb Ellis.

Jimmy's singers were top material as well. After winning a radio talent contest by singing and accompanying himself on four-string guitar, **Bob Eberly** was asked to join the original Dorsey Brothers group when they heard him on a one-niter they were playing in Troy, New York. He got along well with Jimmy, could deliver a pretty ballad as well as an "up tune," and was immensely popular with the fans, placing high on *Billboard*'s Most Popular Male Vocalists lists. Even more popular with the fans was **Helen O'Connell**. They loved her delivery on *tour-de-force* songs and duets with Eberly, but she was equally at home cutting novelty tunes like "Six Lessons from Madame La Zonga" and torchy ballads—and she was extremely pretty. Eberly and O'Connell went on to reprise their duo roles as regulars on TV variety shows.

Bob Wills And His Texas Playboys
"YEARNING (JUST FOR YOU)" 1938

It's called "western swing" now, but **Bob Wills** and His Texas Playboys were definitely part of the big band scene. From his home turf in Texas, Wills wove the sounds of blues, jazz, Latin and *swing* together with a western flair. He cut his musical teeth as a fiddler for barn dances, put together a small group that hit the Texas ballroom circuits, and landed the group some prime, long term radio spots. In the late thirties, Wills expanded the band with the addition of amplified steel guitar, drums, and brass and reed sections. As with any jazz big band, the musicians, especially the guitarists with their renowned, single-note jazz soloing style, took improvised solos, however it was Wills' fiddle that was fundamental to the sound of the band. During the War years, with this full big band complement, Wills enjoyed his biggest chart hits, as well as tremendous popularity on the jukeboxes, and appearances in several motion pictures.

IS IT TRUE WHAT THEY SAY ABOUT DIXIE?

Words & Music by Irving Caesar, Sammy Lerner and Gerald Marks

peo - ple boast, __ And con - sist - ent - ly drink a toast __

To a place __ that a lot of them place __ at the top of the list. __

Are they wrong? __ Are they right? __

Is there rea - son for their de - light? __ I must live in doubt __

SIX LESSONS FROM MADAME LA ZONGA

Words by Charles Newman, Music by James Monaco

Where a ver - y small in - vest - ment _____ pays you div - i - dends ga - lore. _____

Six les - sons _____ from Mad - ame La Zon - ga, _____

You'll do the rhum - ba _____ and the new La Con - ga. _____

Six les - sons _____ in Mad - ame's Ca - ba - na, _____

Interlude

(I'M AFRAID) THE MASQUERADE IS OVER

Words by Herb Magidson, Music by Allie Wrubel

BLUE CHAMPAGNE

Words & Music by Grady Watts, Jimmy Eaton and Frank Ryerson

Blue cham-pagne   Pur-ple shad-ows and Blue cham-pagne   with the ech-oes that

still re-main __   I keep a blue ren-dez-vous. _____

Bub-bles rise __   like a foun-tain be - fore my eyes __   and they sud-den-ly

cryst-al-ize __   to form a vis-ion of you. _____   All the plans we star-ted,

all the songs we sang   each lit-tle dream we knew   seems to o-ver take me

like a boom-er-ang   Blue is the spar-kle   gone is the tang.   Each   old   re-frain ___

Keeps re-turning as   I   re-main ___   With my mem'-ries and   blue cham-pagne

to toast the dream that was you. ___

YEARNING (JUST FOR YOU)

Words & Music by Joe Burke and Benny Davis

*) *Symbols for Guitar, Chords for Ukulele and Banjo*

near_____ smiles have turned to tears_____

_____ Days have turned to years_____

yearn - ing just for you_____ I hope you're yearn -

- - ing too_____ too_____

Horace Heidt And His Orchestra
"GONE WITH THE WIND" 1937
Larry Cotton

There was a piano in every parlor when Horace Heidt was a kid, and he learned to play the one in his home reluctantly. However, he saw how music brought people together at parties or just to sing along, as he did in high school to make new friends. When he was in college, he

fractured a bone in his spine. A friend brought him a phonograph and a stack of records to help him pass the time during his convalescence. The hours he spent listening inspired him to try to make it in the music business. He felt he wasn't good enough to play piano with a pro group, but he reasoned that as a leader he couldn't be fired—so he put together his first five-piece band in 1923. Many bands later, he took a twelve-piece unit into the Palace Theatre in New York, complete with a trained dog named Lobo. A year later the band toured Europe. National recognition came with the *Horace Heidt for Alemite* radio program. Heidt's bands were known for musical gimmicks that delighted his audiences. He knew what was danceable and how to put together a great group of musicians, including electric guitarist Alvino Rey, pianist Frankie Carle, saxophonist and arranger Frank DeVol, and trumpeter Bobby Hackett.

Horace Heidt with an early band and dog Lobo

Many superb singers joined the band including tenor **Larry Cotton**, who appeared in *Billboard's* Most Popular Male Vocalists poll in 1941; Gordon MacRae; and the King Sisters. Heidt knew jazz well, adding many true jazz musicians in the mid forties and booking many famous jazz artists into his own West Coast Trianon Ballroom.

(photo courtesy of Horace Heidt, Jr.)

The 1936 Horace Heidt Orchetra with guitarist Alvino Rey and the King Sisters

Jimmie Lunceford And His Orchestra
"THE FIRST TIME I SAW YOU" 1940
Dan Grissom

When it came to musicianship, this band got the raves—a swing band to the max, jazz musicians to a T, and they were brilliant showmen with highly choreographed moves. Saxophonist Jimmie Lunceford, a meticulous, consistent leader, put

together his first band in Memphis in the late twenties. They received their first radio and recording exposure when they began working a stint at New York's Cotton Club. One of the keys to Lunceford's sound was the arrangements by Sy Oliver. Oliver, a trumpet player, had heard the band in Cincinnati and had asked to write for them. His scores were brilliant, and he later went on to become a top television and film arranger and composer.

The band developed a light, steady swing put forth by musicians such as drummer Jimmie Crawford, saxophonist and vocalist Willie Smith, and trombonist Trummy Young. **Dan Grissom** was the long-term ballad vocalist for the band, good with the sentimental sound but not above a humorous twist. The War and the conditions that a black band had to put up with on the road eventually took their toll, and the band broke up shortly after Lunceford died in 1947.

Jimmie Lunceford

Larry Clinton And His Orchestra
"(I'M AFRAID) THE MASQUERADE IS OVER" 1939
Bea Wain

Larry Clinton made his impact initially as a songwriter and arranger, first with the Dorsey Brothers, then with Jimmy Dorsey, Glen Gray, and Tommy Dorsey. When Clinton established his own band, it was partially with Tommy Dorsey's financial backing as well as support from Eli Oberstein at Victor. Their stint at the Glen Island Casino during the summer of 1938 assured the band's popularity.

Clinton's featured singer was **Bea Wain**, a topflight stylist who had been part of the Kay Thompson Choir. Clinton knew the first time he heard her that she was the right singer, and indeed, the chart-topping standards that they made together form an impressive list. Clinton's prodigious output of recordings relied on a sound that was sweet and an emphasis on pretty tunes.

Joe Venuti And His Orchestra
"CIRIBIRIBIN" 1939
Bing Crosby and the Andrews Sisters

The Andrews Sisters

It was **Joe Venuti** who set the standard for all jazz violinists to come—and that was in the 1920s! During that era, his pairing with guitarist Eddie Lang refined his jazz chops, but he always knew how to swing. He was a featured player with bands such as Red Nichols, Jean Goldkette, and Paul Whiteman's amazing 1929 band that included Benny Goodman and Jack and Charlie Teagarden. Bandleading was not his strong suit, although he attracted talented people such as singer Kay Starr, trumpeter Bobby Hackett, and drummer Barrett Deems.

"Ciribiribin" was recorded with **Bing Crosby**, at the height of his career, and the **Andrews Sisters**, at the beginning of theirs. (The song went on to become the theme song of Harry James.) Crosby, with his group the Rhythm Boys, had his feet in show business and his heart in jazz, and there was only one other singer in the first half of the twentieth century to rival his popularity. With his distinctive, mellow, warm tone, Crosby phrased like a jazz musician—and he could swing at will.

Artie Shaw And His Orchestra
"OH, YOU CRAZY MOON" 1939 • "IMAGINATION" 1940

Artie Shaw

A fine and swinging yet subtle clarinetist, at times rivaling Benny Goodman, Artie Shaw, began his musical career while playing sax in a New Haven, Connecticut high school. He played with various local bands there and in Cleveland, moving to New York to work as a studio musician for CBS and recordings. His break came with his 1936 recordings made with Billie Holiday and Bunny Berigan. In the same year, he formed a big band with strings. In 1937 he changed to a more conventional big band set-up, with a sound featuring a lot of swing and a lot spirit. His singers included Billie Holiday (although she couldn't record with them), Tony Pastor, and Helen Forrest. Soon the band was so popular that the public and press set up a mythical Goodman—Tommy Dorsey—Shaw competition. Though the band was terrific, so was the strain of touring, and Shaw quit abruptly in '39 to regain his failing health—both emotional and physical. Shaw established several bands thereafter, including one for the Navy, all garnering critical acclaim. However, there was a restless, searching nature in Shaw. He kept trying different instrumentation combinations (always hiring the best musicians), studied orchestration, and was continually searching for more musically challenging forms of jazz band. He pursued new band formats into the early fifties, when he left the music business and became a successful author!

THE FIRST TIME I SAW YOU

Words by Allie Wrubel, Music by Nathaniel Shilkret

GONE WITH THE WIND

Flowingly

Music by Allie Wrubel, Words by Herb Magidson

Moderately slow (a tempo)

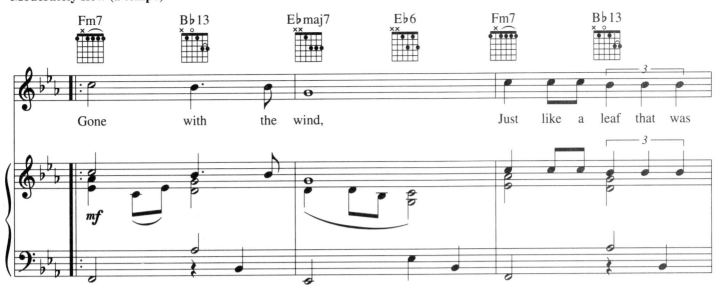

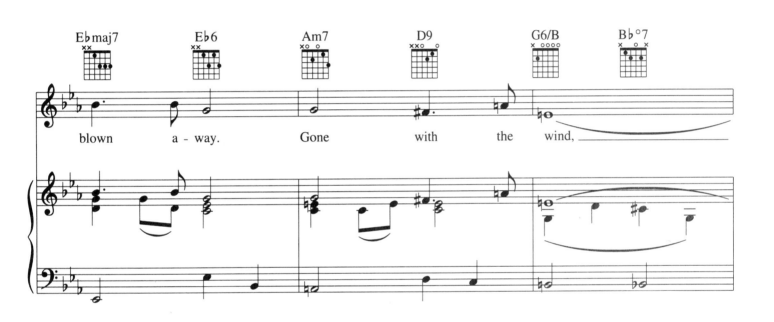

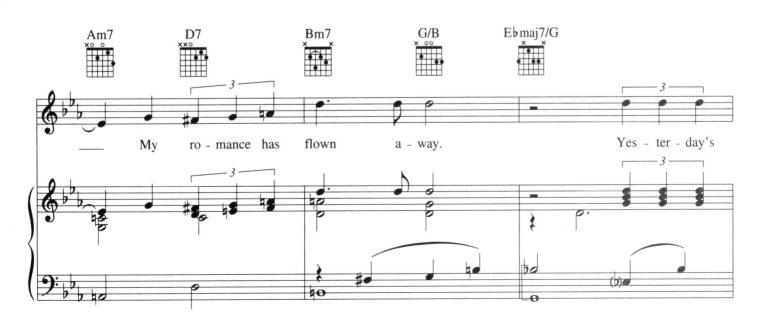

Tommy Dorsey Orchestra 1941, featuring Buddy Rich, Ziggy Elman, Jo Stafford and the Pied Pipers, and Frank Sinatra

Tommy Dorsey
And His Orchestra

"YEARNING (JUST FOR YOU)"* 1938
"OH, YOU CRAZY MOON"* 1939
Jack Leonard
"IMAGINATION" 1940 • "POLKA
DOTS AND MOONBEAMS"
"EVERYTHING HAPPENS TO ME"
"THIS LOVE OF MINE" 1941
"I DREAM OF YOU (MORE THAN
YOU DREAM I DO)" 1945
Frank Sinatra
"LET'S GET AWAY FROM IT ALL" 1941
"IT STARTED ALL OVER AGAIN" 1943
"THERE ARE SUCH THINGS" 1943
Frank Sinatra and the Pied Pipers
"YES INDEED!" 1941
Jo Stafford and Sy Oliver
"WILL YOU STILL BE MINE?" 1944
Connie Haines

When the brothers split, **Tommy Dorsey** went on to establish, arguably, the best swing band in the business. The "Sentimental Gentleman of Swing" and his group could indeed swing and play hot jazz, set many different moods, and excel in many different styles.

Tommy's early forays on trumpet were more influenced by black jazzmen than by Beiderbecke sounds. He switched to solo trombone while in his late twenties during a stint with Paul Whiteman. He continued to solo with the group that he formed with twelve of the personnel of the Joe Haymes band, which had cut their first recordings by September of 1935. Throughout the band's long tenure, Dorsey was able to get the cream of the musicians: Bud Freeman, Bunny Berigan, Louie Bellson, Gene Krupa, Buddy Rich, Charlie Shavers, Max Kaminsky, Buddy De Franco, Ziggy Elman, and Joe Bushkin. Plus, he had the best arrangers in Paul Weston and Axel Stordahl, who handled the pop side, and Sy Oliver and Dean Kincaide, who handled the jazz sounds. Tommy was known as a picky, picky perfectionist whose tantrums were legendary, but those who stayed, including the singers, credit him with contributing in no small way to their own musicalities.

Dorsey's 1939 stellar stable of arrangers Paul Weston and Axel Stordahl with singer Jack Leonard

Jack Leonard was one such singer, who was plucked from a New York band and provided with a perfect setting for a singer. Handsome with a warm personality, he became a bobby-soxer favorite and the Number 1 Male Vocalist in 1939. "Yearning" was an example of a formula that worked for several different numbers, with the band singing hot licks behind the vocalist. Leonard left the band in 1939 after an unfortunate misunderstanding with Dorsey.

As lead singer of the Pied Pipers, **Jo Stafford** could not remember a time when she wasn't singing, starting off first in a trio with her two older sisters as the Stafford Sisters. Ray Charles said her voice had "a silky quality" and a haunting style.

When Stafford joined the **Pied Pipers,** they were an octet. Two of the King Sisters told their current dates, Paul Weston (whom Stafford later married) and Axel Stordahl, about the group. Dorsey auditioned them for a half-hour radio show and kept them for two months, but eventually decided that he couldn't afford eight singers. Later, when the group became a quartet, he rehired them. Stafford became the solo ballad singer, singing many of the arrangements by **Sy Oliver**. That was in 1939; shortly afterward, Sinatra joined Dorsey in the slot left open by Leonard and fit in well as a solo singer with the group. Stafford sensed his uniqueness immediately.

Dorsey heard **Frank Sinatra** when he was singing with Harry James in Chicago. Dorsey offered Sinatra a job, which he promptly took. Sinatra's wife was due to have a baby, and James, who could not pay as well as Dorsey, was kind enough to let Sinatra go. Sinatra wowed the audience the minute he appeared with the Dorsey band. If they thought that Leonard was a bobby-soxer favorite, they weren't prepared for Sinatra's kind of appeal. After Sinatra's first week, Dorsey predicted he'd be as big as Crosby (what prescience!). Dorsey did his best to provide a comfortable setting for his singers, and was a good teacher, helping Sinatra develop his phrasing (which in large part was copied from Dorsey's trombone phrasing), breathing, and musical taste and style. Sinatra was eager to learn, to improve and broaden his talents.

Songwriter Matt Dennis ["Everything Happens to Me" and "Let's Get Away from It All"]

Sinatra's rise to popularity was swift. He had sung in the high school glee clubs in Hoboken, New Jersey, and was inspired to become a professional singer when he saw Bing Crosby perform in a 1936 concert. His group, the Hoboken Four, won the *Major Bowes Original Amateur Radio Hour* in 1937, and by 1939 he was singing on eighteen different local radio shows in the greater New York area—mostly without pay. After his short stint with Harry James, and within a few months of joining Dorsey, the hits began to flow. Sinatra had his first jaunt onto the *Billboard* charts with "Polka Dots and Moonbeams" by Johnny Burke and Jimmy Van Heusen, and with "Everything Happens to Me" and "Let's Get Away from It All" from the sometimes quirky, sometimes romantic pen of Matt Dennis. (There would be many more Sinatra hits from these writers in the future.) The combination of Sinatra and Dorsey, plus Stafford, the Pied Pipers, and the incredible musicians in the band made the Dorsey band Number 1 on the college, male singer, and band popularity polls in the early forties. In 1942, after the record-breaking engagement at the Paramount Theater in New York where thousands of swooning teenagers made the newsreels, Sinatra decided to strike out on his own.

The Tommy Dorsey band continued at the peak until late 1946, when they joined the growing ranks of retiring bands. However, Dorsey was not one to sit back and relax. Two years later he was back with an impressive band, and he was smart enough to get a variety show on TV, where he introduced two new stars—Connie Francis and Elvis Presley. He also reunited with Jimmy, who joined his band and took over its leadership after his death.

Tommy Dorsey Orchestra 1941 with Dorsey on trombone, Frank Sinatra center and Jo Stafford and the Pied Pipers next to the flag

Bands in the Big Band Era didn't last long unless the leaders were both consummate musicians and topflight businesspersons. Tommy Dorsey met both criteria—big time. He did take gambles and occasionally got burned, but he built some empire. Besides his bands, one of his best investments was in his music publishing companies—Embassy and Sun. You'll find that a major percentage of the music in this collection emanates from those catalogues.

IMAGINATION

Words & Music by Johnny Burke and Jimmy Van Heusen

+Symbols for Guitar, Chords for Ukulele and Banjo

CIRIBIRIBIN

English version by Irving Bibo, Words by Rudolf Thaler, Music by Alberto Pestalozza

OH! YOU CRAZY MOON

Words & Music by Johnny Burke and Jimmy Van Heusen

Refrain (Slowly with expression)

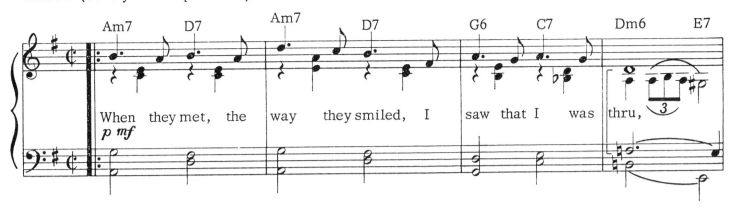

When they met, the way they smiled, I saw that I was thru,

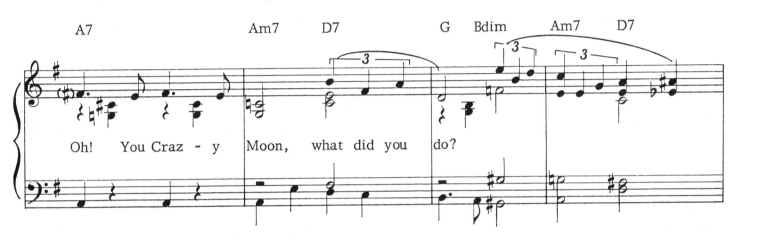

Oh! You Craz - y Moon, what did you do?

When they kissed, they tried to say That it was just in fun,

Oh! You Craz - y Moon, look what you've done!

Once you prom-ised me, you know, that it would nev-er end,____ You should be a-

shamed to show_ your fun-ny face, my friend;__ There they are, they fell in love, I

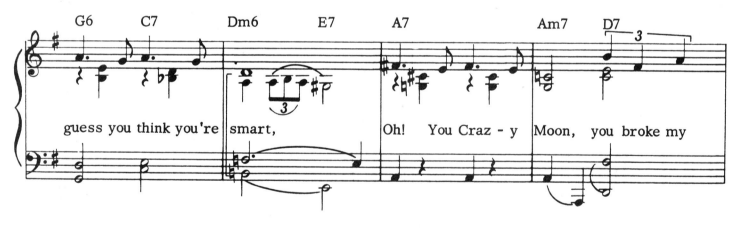

guess you think you're smart, Oh! You Craz-y Moon, you broke my

heart.__

heart.__

rit.

Count Basie And His Orchestra
"POLKA DOTS AND MOONBEAMS" • "THERE ARE SUCH THINGS" 1940

New Jersey born **William 'Count' Basie** learned piano from the finest: James P. Johnson and Fats Waller. He toured on the vaudeville circuit, settling in Kansas City. There he took over the remnants of the Bennie Moten Kansas City Orchestra, forming them into his own group, the Barons of Rhythm. His break came when producer John Hammond heard a radio broadcast of the group and flew to Kansas City with booker Willard Alexander to sign them. The band did some touring and took its first major booking at New York's Roseland Ballroom. Their sound: big, full and swinging, and musically accessible to the big band-loving public.

The Count not only attracted some of the world's best jazz musicians—Harry Edison, Clark Terry, Thad Jones, Lester Young, Illinois Jacquet, Bennie Powell, Eddie Davis—but over the years he also hired the best singers, including Billie Holiday, Jimmy Rushing, Helen Humes, and Joe Williams. His arranger alumni include Neal Hefti, Benny Carter, and Sammy Nestico. Basie and his bands kept right on grooving, touring worldwide until his death in 1984. The band has continued to perform to this day with Basie's marvelous charts to guide them.

Count Basie

Kay Kyser And His Orchestra
"WHY DON'T WE DO THIS MORE OFTEN?" 1941
Ginny Simms and Harry Babbitt

Here's a guy who knew how to get people's interest. To keep his Chicago-based radio program on the air in 1934, he came up with a gimmick: **Kay Kyser**'s College of Musical Knowledge—a kind of "name that tune" contest for the audience. The response was so great that he got a network radio show out of it. He ran a tight band, hiring players with all-around good habits, who stuck with him for a long time. Nonetheless, they had a good time playing both novelties like "Chatterbox" and danceable tunes. Kyser dedicated much of the band's time during the war years to play in armed-services camps and hospitals.

Harry Babbitt and **Ginny Sims** were with Kyser in those early war years. Babbitt was known for his consistently good vocal presentation, and he caught everybody with his warm smile. Beauteous Sims, who started out along with Tony Martin and Woody Herman in Tom Gerun's band in the early thirties, was known for her lyrical interpretations. She was so popular in 1941 that she was voted the Number 1 Female Band Vocalist in *Billboard*'s college poll. After appearing in several movies, she went on to host radio and television shows in the early fifties.

Kay Kyser in "College of Musical Knowledge" garb.

POLKA DOTS AND MOONBEAMS

Words & Music by Johnny Burke and Jimmy Van Heusen

EVERYTHING HAPPENS TO ME

Words & Music by Tom Adair and Matt Dennis

tel - e - graphed and phoned, I sent an "Air - mail Spec - ial" too,   Your

ans - wer was "Good - by," And there was ev - en pos - tage due,   I

fell in love just once and then it had to be with you ___

EV - 'RY - THING HAP - PENS TO ME ___   I ___

YES INDEED!

Words & Music by Sy Oliver

131

LET'S GET AWAY FROM IT ALL

Words & Music by Matt Dennis and Tom Adair

town to town, __ We'll vis - it ev - 'ry state I'll re - peat "I

love you, Sweet!" In all the for - ty eight. __ Let's go a - gain __ to Ni - a -

- g'ra __ this time we'll look __ at the "Fall" __ Let's leave our hut, __ Dear, Get

out of our rut, __ Dear, Let's get a - way __ from it all. __

IT STARTED ALL OVER AGAIN

Words by Bill Carey, Music by Carl Fischer

THERE ARE SUCH THINGS

Words & Music by Stanley Adams, Abel Baer and George Meyer

THIS LOVE OF MINE

Words & Music by Frank Sinatra, Sol Parker and Henry Sanicola

WILL YOU STILL BE MINE

Words by Tom Adair, Music by Matt Dennis

Chorus

When lov-ers make no ren-dez-vous ____ To stroll a - long Fifth Av-en-ue ____ When this fa - mil-iar world is thru ____ Will you still be mine? ____ When cabs don't drive a-round the park ____ No win-dows light the sum-mer dark ____ When love has lost its sec-ret spark ____ Will you still be mine? ____

I DREAM OF YOU
(MORE THAN YOU DREAM I DO)

Words by Edna Osser, Music by Marjorie Goetchius

Glenn Miller And His Orchestra
"I'M STEPPING OUT WITH A MEMORY TONIGHT" 1940
"IMAGINATION" 1940
Ray Eberle
"TUXEDO JUNCTION" 1940
Glenn Miller and His Orchestra

Glenn Miller

(From the collection of Ian Whitcomb)

It seems that whenever anyone wants to evoke the aura of the Big Band Era, he or she merely has to put on a **Glenn Miller** recording. Yet this leader's superbly polished band was around for only eight years. Miller began his career as a jazz trombonist and arranger for the bands of Ben Pollack, Red Nichols, the Dorsey brothers, Glen Gray, Benny Goodman, and finally Ray Noble. When Miller went out on his own in 1937, he had a tough time getting going—the problems were typical of many fledgling groups: not enough money for experienced musicians, musicians who drank themselves into stupors, booking problems, and finding just the right groove. Somehow it all came together in 1939: Miller found his trademark reed sound and a group of musicians that impressed the management of the Glen Island Casino enough to book the band for the summer, therefore providing them the necessary radio exposure. Miller was also smart enough to sign on with Bluebird—Victor's less expensive label—and cut a lot of recordings (not all of the big bands were so hot to record; they felt that they got more income from live performances). Miller also found arrangers who could take over some of his duties and provide musical variety. Preeminent among these was Bill Finegan, who was later associated with the popular Sauter-Finegan Orchestra, and Billy May, who was also the lead trumpeter.

Amusingly, Miller found **Ray Eberle** when he jokingly inquired of the much-admired Bob Eberly if he "had a brother at home." Sure enough he did, even though he (Bob) now spelled his last name differently. Although Ray was no singer when he started out, Miller helped him become one so popular that Ray beat out his brother Bob—and even Sinatra—on

most of the *Billboard* polls in the early forties. His romantic-ballad delivery was well matched to the band's sound, and he appeared on hit after charting hit until his departure in 1942.

Later in '42, though he was beyond draft age, Miller enlisted in the Air Force. There he put together an aggregate of talented draftees—the finest musicians, singers, and arrangers from many of the big bands. They rehearsed at Yale University, played some unique marching-band arrangements, and did a series of weekly Air Force recruitment shows that were broadcast nationally. When the overseas orders arrived, the group found themselves based in Bedford, England, where they broadcast over the BBC daily and played concerts for service personnel throughout the country. On December 15, Miller took an unscheduled flight to Paris to prepare for some future gigs there. He never arrived, and no trace of his plane was ever found.

WHY DON'T WE DO THIS MORE OFTEN?

Words by Charles Newman, Music by Allie Wrubel

153

make each oth - er laugh, we make each oth - er sing, And

you can nev - er, ev - er o - ver-do a good thing. _____ So

why don't we do _____ this more of - ten?

Just what we're do - ing to - night. night.

Jan Savitt And His Orchestra
"TUXEDO JUNCTION" 1940
Allan DeWitt

A bandleader with an unlikely background for playing swing was **Jan Savitt**. At the age six in his native Russia, Savitt was lauded as a child prodigy on violin. At fifteen, after he had come to the U.S., he was awarded three scholarships to Curtis Institute for playing and conducting, and he became the youngest musician ever to play in the Philadelphia Orchestra. By 1926, he had assembled a musical group; soon had his own network radio series; and his swing group, the Top Hatters, began getting national attention. Savitt easily grasped the complexities of jazz, and his command of the music's nuances showed in the band's output.

Savitt had several band singers including Bon Bon (George Tunnell), one of the first African Americans to sing with a white band. On Savitt's recording of "Tuxedo Junction," the vocal chores fell to **Alan DeWitt**, who had sung with the Tommy Dorsey Band. The song was on the charts three times in 1940, but it was the instrumental version by Glenn Miller that hit Number 1.

Jan Savitt

Gene Krupa And His Orchestra
"JUST A LITTLE BIT SOUTH OF NORTH CAROLINA" 1941
Anita O'Day
"LET ME OFF UPTOWN" 1941
Anita O'Day and Roy Eldridge

There was probably no more energetic personality in the form of a bandleader than **Gene Krupa**. He brought the drum set to the public's notice, demonstrating its validity as a solo jazz instrument. Starting with his stint with Benny Goodman in the mid thirties, he had innumerable hit recordings as a featured performer (with Goodman and various other groups) throughout the thirties, forties, and fifties. He formed his own first-class band in 1938, highlighting his own talents as well as those of Roy Eldridge on trumpet and Anita O'Day's vocals.

Anita O'Day named as her influences Mildred Bailey, Ella Fitzgerald, Billie Holiday, and, of all people, Martha Ray (in her stint with Earl Hines). Her first singing gigs were in Chicago clubs; her big break came when she replaced Irene Day in Krupa's band in 1941. Many feel that her inventive jazz style helped push Krupa's band to a new level of musicianship. Her duo with trumpeter **Roy Eldridge** on "Let Me Off Uptown" was one of the band's biggest hits. The recording showed off the sensational soloing talents of both artists and enjoyed a twelve-week stay on the pop charts. O'Day moved on to the Stan Kenton Band in 1944.

Blessed with an innate sense of rhythm, critics have always raved about Anita O'Day's interpretation, her inventiveness, and her improvisational skills. Hers is an instrumental voice; that is, she uses it like one of the instruments in the band. She was probably the first white woman to scat sing.

Gene Krupa

Singer Anita O'Day

TUXEDO JUNCTION

Words & Music by Erskine Hawkins, William Johnson, Julian Dash and Buddy Feyne

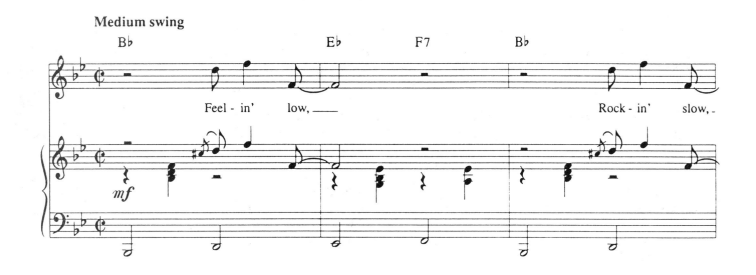

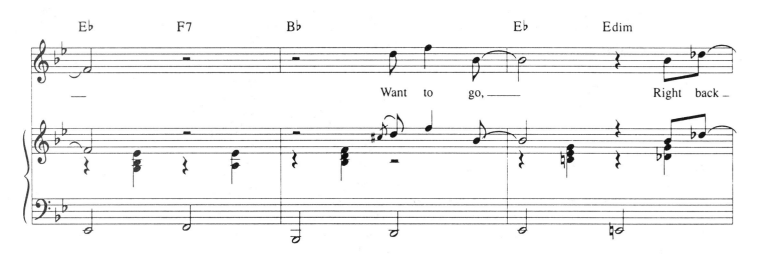

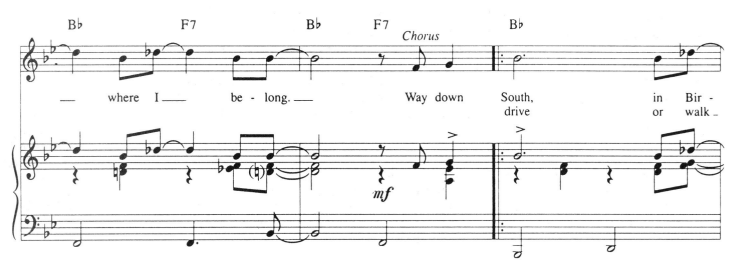

I'M STEPPING OUT
WITH A MEMORY TONIGHT

Words by Herb Magidson, Music by Allie Wrubel

161

do. _____ I'll dine at the old ca-fé where we had so much fun, And or-der cock-tails for two in-stead of the u-su-al one. Then af-ter dark ___ in a han-som through the

Sammy Kaye And His Orchestra

"DADDY" 1941
Kaye Choir
"I'M A BIG GIRL NOW" 1946
Betty Barclay
"RED SILK STOCKINGS AND GREEN PERFUME" 1947
Don Cornell

Sammy Kaye

"Swing and sway with **Sammy Kaye**" was probably the best slogan of the Big Band Era. And swing he did: He knew exactly how to take the pulse of the public and program a swinging set that would keep the dancers happy with nary a break. He ran a tight band—polished, rehearsed, and up on the latest sounds. He also knew how to highlight his concerts by bringing in major guest stars like Teddy Wilson, Roy Eldridge, and Gene Krupa. Kaye liked to feature his vocalists, and he had many—including his own **Kaye Choir** who were featured on his Number 1 chart hit "Daddy," written by a young, hip Bobby Troup. The most successful of Kaye's singers was smooth-voiced **Don Cornell,** who went solo with big hits in the fifties.

Harry James And His Orchestra

"WAITIN' FOR THE TRAIN TO COME IN" 1945
Kitty Kallen

Harry James started out in Ben Pollack's band. He was twenty years old in 1936, and he'd been playing trumpet in dance bands since his early teens. The critics raved about his hot, wild, and enthusiastic style, and by the end of 1936 he was in Benny Goodman's band—having a ball and well liked by everyone. When James established his own band in 1939, Goodman even invested money in it. It was a great swing band, but James never forgot the importance of danceable tempos.

Harry James with wife Betty Grable and Willie Smith

While listening to a radio broadcast in New York featuring Harold Arden's Band beaming from the Rustic Cabin in Englewood, New Jersey, James heard a singer he liked. He didn't get the singer's name and so he had to cross the river to find him. When he found Frank Sinatra, he signed him. Sinatra stayed for only a few years. The band played a stint in Los Angeles that didn't work out too well and then moved on to Chicago. Here, Tommy Dorsey offered Sinatra a job, and James gracefully let him out of his contract.

The band continued to grow musically, as did James with his "hot" trumpeting. He hired sidemen such as Sam Donahue and Claude Lakey and vocalists Dick Haymes and Helen Forrest. The emotional and musical give and take between Forrest and James increased their popularity and record sales, and by 1942 they were considered the most popular band in the country.

In the summer of 1943, James married top wartime movie star Betty Grable and was declared 4-F (medically unfit for service) by the draft board. They tried again to draft him in 1944, but he was still 4-F. The news that James might have to go to war wreaked havoc on the band's personnel. Nonetheless, Harry re-formed the band with great success, and the moment that the recording ban was lifted in late 1944, he cut a group of songs with his new singer **Kitty Kallen.** Kallen was a consistent, excellent singer who had been in the short-lived Jack Teagarden band in 1939, moving on to Jimmy Dorsey's band at its height. In 1946, after her stint with James, she moved on to Artie Shaw's band. She also had a string of pop hits in the fifties.

LET ME OFF UPTOWN

Words & Music by Redd Evans and Earl Bostic

JUST A LITTLE BIT SOUTH
OF NORTH CAROLINA

Words & Music by Sunny Skylar, Arthur Shaftel and Bette Cannon

weath-er's fine ___ and the folks are feel - in' great, that the

gar - den looks grand, and the red rose vine ___ is cling - ing to the

gate. Just a lit - tle bit south of North Car - o - li - na,

that's where my thoughts all stray. To the one I love best in

Al Trace And His Orchestra
"MAIRZY DOATS" 1944
Red Maddock

Al Trace's recording of "Mairzy Doats" was his first foray on the charts as a bandleader. Oddly, the big recording of "Mairzy Doats" by the Merry Macs appeared on the charts two weeks later than Trace's and stayed on the charts simultaneously. Trace's real claim to fame was his songwriting skill. His biggest recordings to hit the charts were "You Call Everybody Darlin'" and the comedic song "If I Knew You Were Comin' I'd've Baked a Cake," recorded by Eileen Barton, Georgia Gibbs, and a multitude of others.

Stan Kenton And His Orchestra
"TAMPICO" 1945
June Christy

"Different, energetic, a big sound and definitely swinging jazz"—all the things **Stan Kenton** was when the band debuted in 1941. Reviewers noted positively his unique combina-

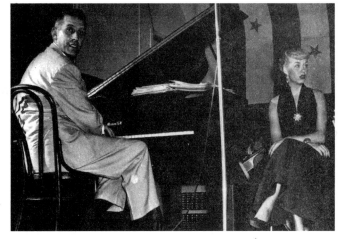

tions of instrumental voicings and rhythm with emphasis on the words "hard-hitting," "big," and "full." Kenton, a pianist who had played in Everett Hoagland's and Gus Arnheim's orchestras, hired an exciting group of top musicians of the time. These included bassist Howard Rumsey, drummer Shelly Manne, trombonist Kai Winding, and tenor saxophonists Vido Musso and Stan Getz. His musicians praised and respected him—they loved the challenge of his original arrangements and his sound. When Pete Rugolo joined up as arranger, his distinctive form of arranging gave new shape to the band's sound and provided Kenton with time to write. Indeed, the band went on to become the forerunners of progressive jazz.

Stan Kenton accompanying singer June Christy
(Photo from the Stan Kenton collection courtesy of California State University, Los Angeles)

In 1945, **June Christy** succeeded **Anita O'Day** as Kenton's band singer. She had established herself as a well-liked big-band singer while working with society bands in Chicago, including those of Boyd Raeburn, Benny Storey, and Denny Beckner. She appeared on all of Kenton's chart hits from 1945 to 1948, and married his saxophonist Bob Cooper. When Kenton's band changed (as it often did) in the late forties, she went solo, occasionally appearing with Kenton's new bands, Bob Cooper, or Pete Rugolo.

Vaughn Monroe And His Orchestra
"THERE! I'VE SAID IT AGAIN" 1945
Vaughn Monroe

He wanted to be an opera singer, but the Depression prevented him from financing his lessons, so **Vaughn Monroe** built up his trumpet chops and got into the big-band business. He was savvy enough to give the customers what they wanted musically, plus his romantic baritone voice and good looks were an additional draw. His band debuted on the charts in 1940 with a Number 1 hit, and they continued to stay on the charts throughout the forties. They too had an outstanding arranger in the person of Ray Conniff. Monroe got a copy of "There I've Said It Again" in 1941 from songwriter Redd Evans. When he finally recorded it in 1945, it sold three and a half million copies.

Vaughn Monroe

I'M A BIG GIRL NOW

Words & Music by Jerry Livingston, Milton Drake and Al Hoffman

both of us were three. There's a change in my talk-ing, there's a

change in my walk-ing, He ought to take a good look at me. ___ I'm a

Moderately slow, a tempo

big girl now, ___ I wan-na be treat-ed like a big girl now. _____
big girl now, ___ I wan-na be cud-dled like a big girl now. _____
big girl now, ___ I wan-na be thrill-ing like a big girl now. _____
big girl now, ___ I wan-na go plac-es like a big girl now. _____
big girl now, ___ I wan-na be dar-ing like a big girl now. _____

RED SILK STOCKINGS AND GREEN PERFUME

Words & Music by Dick Sanford, Bob Hilliard and Sammy Mysels

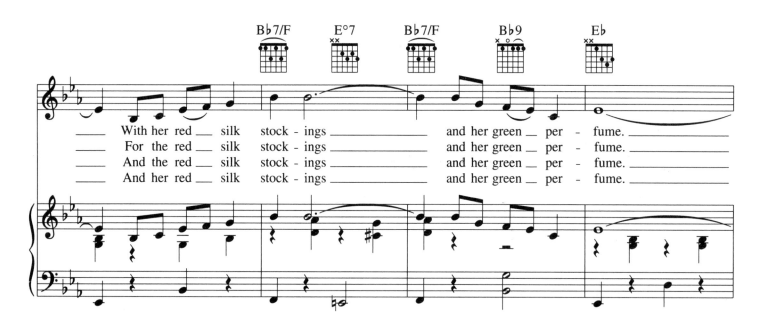

Oh, the town was grow-in' and the mon-ey was flow-in' And the
boys were throw-in' it a - round For the red ___ silk stock - ings ___
___ and the green ___ per - fume. ___

1.,2.,3.
2. She ar - rived on a
3. She was sing - in' a
4. Though she prom-ised to

4.
fume.

WAITIN' FOR THE TRAIN TO COME IN

Words & Music by Martin Block and Sunny Skylar

DADDY

Words & Music by Bobby Troup

sa-bles. clothes with Pa - ris la - bels Dad - dy!

You ought-a get the best for me. _____

Here's 'na - maz - ing re - vel - a - tion With a bit of

stim-u - la - tion. I'd be a great sen - sa - tion,

Johnny Long And His Orchestra
"WAITIN' FOR THE TRAIN TO COME IN"   1945
Dick Robertson

A charming guy, and a left-handed violinist, **Johnny Long** had a fine, musical, sweet-sounding band—the kind to which people loved to dance. Before joining Long, soft-voiced **Dick Robertson** had had a long career as a band singer, showing up in the early thirties with the Ipana Troubadours (of which the Dorsey brothers were also members), Ben Selvin's much-recorded orchestra, and Victor Young's orchestra. He then established his own group with some top musicians (including Bobby Hackett) and garnered quite a string of chart hits.

*An original sheet music cover
with a duo of artists who also "covered" the song*

Les Brown And His Orchestra
"AREN'T YOU GLAD YOU'RE YOU" 1946
Doris Day

Clarinetist **Les Brown**'s band started out at Duke University calling themselves the Duke Blue Devils. Instead of finishing school, they took off for the road, landing a summer job at the Playland Casino in Rye, New York. This venue was the first major gig for a lot of big bands on their way up. When the summer was over, the group disbanded and most of the players returned to school, but Brown continued to write and arrange for other known bands. During a 1938 stint fronting his own band, he caught the attention of RCA Victor's chief of A&R (Artists and Repertoire), Eli Oberstein, who got him a booking in the Green Room in New York City's Edison Hotel. Their popularity grew, their musicianship was legendary—they were considered a band of "musicians' musicians." The members were so happy to be working together that they regularly turned down offers to play in bigger name groups.

Les Brown

Many remember **Doris Day** as the wholesome, peppy star of many a fifties sugarcoated movie. However, this scrub-faced chirper was originally discovered by Bob Crosby, whose band she soon left to join up with Brown's group at the tender age of seventeen. The professionalism of the group along with Day's easy-going nature, plus her natural feel and voice, proved a winning combination. Her stay there was also fairly short (she left to get married), but she was grateful for the break. Brown got Day to rejoin the band in 1945 by providing room for her mother and her son at the hotel. "Aren't You Glad You're You" was first heard sung by Bing Crosby in the 1945 film *The Bells of Saint Mary's*.

Singer Doris Day

THERE! I'VE SAID IT AGAIN

Words & Music by Redd Evans and Dave Mann

MAIRZY DOATS

Words & Music by Al Hoffman, Milton Drake and Jerry Livingston

TAMPICO

Words & Music by Allan Roberts and Doris Fisher

Tam - pi - co, Tam - pi - co, on the Gulf of Me - hi - co,

Tam - pi - co, Tam - pi - co, that's the place for you to go.

Tam - pi - co, Tam - pi - co, where ba - nan - a boats all go,

Tam - pi - co, Tam - pi - co, down in Me - hi - co. 1. If

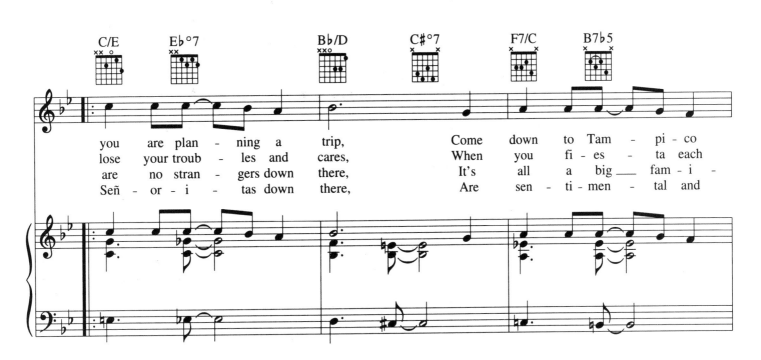

you are plan - ning a trip, Come down to Tam - pi - co
lose your troub - les and cares, When you fi - es - ta each
are no stran - gers down there, It's all a big___ fam - i -
Señ - or - i - tas down there, Are sen - ti - men - tal and

Tex Beneke And His Orchestra
"MY HEART IS A HOBO" 1947
Mello Larks

Beneke was one of those talented 'doublers.' He not only sang, he played tenor sax. He joined Glenn Miller's Orchestra in 1938 just as Miller's star was rising. Miller showed his appreciation of Tex's abilities by giving him a variety of interesting solo opportunities with the band. After Miller died, Beneke took over the leadership of the band—and did an extremely creditable job. However, Victor records wanted the sound of the Miller band to remain the same, while Tex wanted to shape the band's sound and let it develop and mature, as he felt that Miller would have done. So, Beneke left to form his own band—along the way hiring an unknown arranger by the name of Henry Mancini.

Sam Donahue And His Orchestra
"DO YOU CARE?" 1947
Irene Daye

Known as a good leader as well as a powerful sax player, **Sam Donahue** formed his first band in Detroit in the early forties. When offered a job with Gene Krupa, he turned the band over to Sonny Burke, and then later took it back. He began turning it into an impressive unit, only to get drafted. Joining the Navy, he took over Artie Shaw's band and turned that unit into a first-rate band as well, one that fortunately left several recordings. He set up another band after the war, but bookings were difficult to come by. In the sixties, Donahue took over Tommy Dorsey's band.

A fine and pretty singer, **Irene Daye** sang with Gene Krupa and was featured on several of his major recordings. She was pursued by both trumpet player Corky Cornelius and saxophonist Sam Donahue. Cornelius won her hand and took her with him to the Casa Loma orchestra, though later Donahue got her to record with him. When Cornelius died, Irene joined Charlie Spivak's band, eventually marrying him.

AREN'T YOU GLAD YOU'RE YOU

Words by Johnny Burke, Music by Jimmy Van Heusen

Verse: Do you make the most of your five sen-ses, or is your life like Old Moth-er Hub-bard's shelf? Well, mark this on your slate, life is not an emp-ty plate, that's if you ap-pre-ci-ate your-self.

Tony Pastor And His Orchestra
"THE LADY FROM 29 PALMS" 1947
"RED SILK STOCKINGS AND GREEN PERFUME" 1947
Tony Pastor
"'A'—YOU'RE ADORABLE" 1949
Rosemary and Betty Clooney

Tony Pastor's early playing years were interwoven with Artie Shaw's. They played together in several bands when they were both in New Haven. When Shaw formed his own band in 1936, he asked Pastor to join as sax player and one of his vocalists. When Shaw abruptly ran off to Mexico, Pastor took up band booker Si Shribman's offer of backing and started his own band. A long booking at the Blue Room at New York's Hotel Lincoln gave the new band a major break with continual weekly radio play. From good swing and dance music they evolved into a jazz unit by the mid forties, but the group always had a warm sound generated by Pastor's own sax playing, singing, and personality. Both "The Lady from 29 Palms" and "Red Silk Stockings and Green Perfume" were multiple Top 10 chart hits in 1947, each covered by major big bands or artists.

Tony Pastor

Aside from Pastor, the band's most famous singer was **Rosemary Clooney**, a fine, earthy jazz singer who started with him at age seventeen. She was brought up on big-band music, listening to it on the nickel jukeboxes at home in Cincinnati. Clooney started her career while still in high school by setting up an audition for herself and her sister for a radio show that eventually brought them to Pastor's attention.

Russ Morgan And His Orchestra
"CRUISING DOWN THE RIVER" 1949
Skylarks

Would starting in the business by arranging for John Philip Sousa and Victor Herbert be a good background for a big-band leader? For **Russ Morgan** these experiences were but one part of a large and varied musical background that included playing trombone with the Detroit Symphony, the Jean Goldkette Orchestra, the Dorsey Brothers Orchestra, and Fletcher Henderson; serving as recording director of the American Record Company; acting as NBC staff conductor; and more. He developed his signature "wah-wah" sound on trombone while with Freddy Martin's band and kept it on while playing with his own band—a group with a sweet, light blend. Not only were his arranging skills excellent, but he was a consistently good songwriter ("You're Nobody 'Til Somebody Loves You," "Does Your Heart Beat for Me?").

Russ Morgan

The **Skylarks** were Morgan's vocal group, working with him in the late forties and then going out on their own for a brief foray on the charts. "Cruising Down the River" was one of four Morgan recordings that were in the Top 10 simultaneously in 1949.

DO YOU CARE?

Words & Music by Jack Elliott and Lew Quadling

Do you care? _____ Is there a chance for me? _____ Do you

care? _____ I wish I knew; _____ Won't you try to con-fess _____

That you find hap-i-ness _____ In a ten-der ca-ress _____

_____ The way I do? _____ Do you care? _____

MY HEART IS A HOBO

Words by Johnny Burke, Music by Jimmy Van Heusen

Moderately a tempo, with a tilt

THE LADY FROM 29 PALMS

Words & Music by Allie Wrubel

LA-DY FROM TWEN-TY NINE PALMS. ——— She's a Yip! yip! yip-py-aye dol-ly, A new kind a gal of the west. And Yip! Yip! Yip-py by gol-ly! ——

What-ev-er she does she does the best ——— She got twen-ty nine di-'mond rings.
She makes you hap-py when you're de-pressed!

——— Got 'em with-out an-y strings She is a dy-na-mite dream-boat A load of a-tom bombs THE LA-DY FROM TWEN-TY NINE PALMS. She left PALMS.

213

"A" – YOU'RE ADORABLE

Words & Music by Buddy Kaye, Fred Wise and Sid Lippman

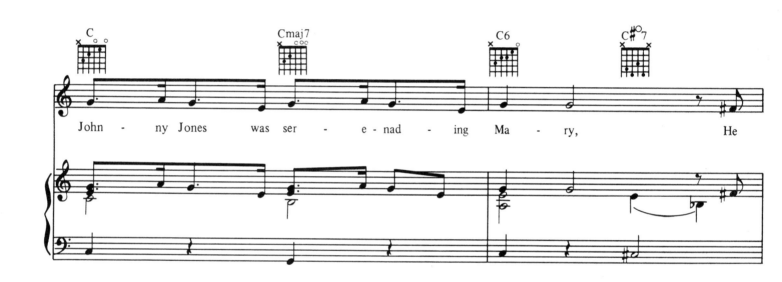

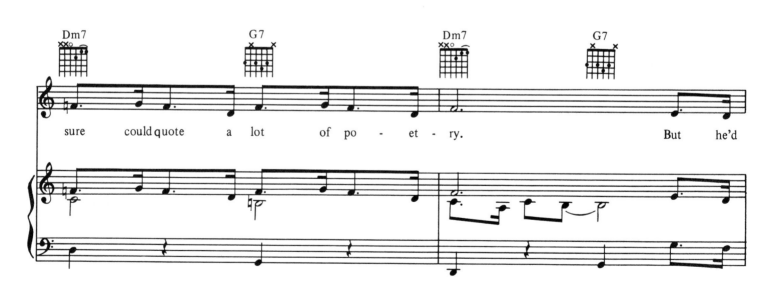

much rath - er tell 'er what he learned in his spell - er when they

both at - ten - ded P. S. Thir - ty - three.

Chorus:

"A" you're a - dor - a - ble, "B" you're so beau - ti - ful, "C" you're a cu - tie full o'

charms. "D" you're a dar - ling, and "E" you're ex - cit - ing, and

CRUISING DOWN THE RIVER

Words & Music by Eily Beadell and Nell Tollerton

Cruis - ing Down The Riv - er, _____ on a Sun - day

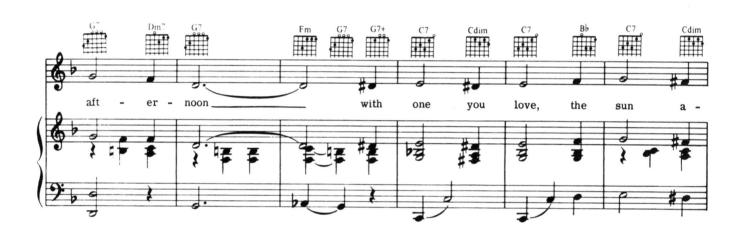

aft - er - noon _____ with one you love, the sun a -

bove wait - ing for the moon. _____ The old ac -

make a sound like soft - ly fall - ing rain._____ Just

two of us to - geth - er,_____ we'll plan a hon - ey -

moon_____ Cruis - ing Down The Riv - er,_____ on a

Sun - day aft - er noon. noon._____

Duke Ellington And His Famous Orchestra

"TAKE THE 'A' TRAIN" 1952
Betty Roche
"COME SUNDAY" (1944) 1958
Mahalia Jackson
"SATIN DOLL" (1953) 1963
Alice Babs

When it came to jazz in the big-band idiom, it was **Duke Ellington** who invented the art form. He was born in Washington, D.C., where he started studying piano at age seven and began playing professionally while still in high school. He played with numerous bands there, in New York (purportedly, he moved to New York at the urging of Fats Waller), and on the road. He had formed his first jazz band by 1923, a larger group two years later, and took up residency at Harlem's renowned Cotton Club in 1927, leaving there to tour in 1931.

Duke Ellington

When his big band came into its own in the thirties, he enjoyed respect and popularity in Europe as well as in the States. His was the best jazz big band ever. In later years, he was seen as a musical statesman for the U.S., receiving worldwide acclaim. (As good as they were—certainly better than most any other group, and known for their extremely classy, well-turned-out appearance—it took a while for Ellington's band to be booked into the more prestigious locales stateside.) Hollywood called as well, with several plum film appearances.

During the thirties, Ellington was unique among big-band leaders in that he consistently wrote for his band, with many of his tunes destined to become hits and then standards. (His tune "It Don't Mean a Thing if It Ain't Got That Swing" contributed to naming the Swing Era.) He was the first composer to write successful extended jazz compositions. From 1943 to 1950, his annual concerts at Carnegie Hall introduced a series of longer works. "Come Sunday" comes from one such work, *Black, Brown, and Beige.* He planned it as "a tone poem parallel to the history of the American Negro," and felt that "a statement of social protest in the theater should be made without saying it." It was premiered at Carnegie Hall in 1943, but because of the recording ban, it was never recorded in its entirety.

Like Benny Goodman, Ellington had the knack for securing the talents of the finest jazz musicians to join him on recordings as well as in the band. Cootie Williams, Ben Webster, Harry Carney, Johnny Hodges, Barney Bigard, Louis Bellson, and Clark Terry were among those who fit into this category. Often, Ellington's compositions were tailored to the soloing chops of these particular musicians, though "freedom of expression" was a byword of the Ellington groups. The addition of arranger/pianist/composer Billy Strayhorn (lyricist with Johnny Mercer on "Satin Doll," lyric and music on "Take The 'A' Train") in the late thirties added another level of creativity to the group.

Throughout Ellington's long career, he had a fine array of singers: Ivie Anderson in the early days, baritone Herb Jeffries (one of the first black cowboy stars), Al Hibbler, Billy Strayhorn, Kay Davis, and Ray Nance. He showed his inventiveness early on by having his vocalist Adelaide Hall use her voice wordlessly as an instrument. **Betty Roche** gained the attention of various big band leaders by winning an amateur singing contest at the Apollo. She joined Duke Ellington in 1943, and sang the "Blues" segment of *Black, Brown, and Beige* later that year. She left Ellington the following year, and rejoined the band in 1952, when she recorded the most renowned vocal version of "…'A' Train."

Ellington and his band continued to perform throughout the world until his death in 1974. He made more recordings than anyone else in jazz, and is considered one the twentieth century's finest composers.

SATIN DOLL

Music by Duke Ellington, Words by Billy Strayhorn and Johnny Mercer

out skip-pin'   care-ful a - mi - go,   you're flip-pin'

Speaks Lat - in   that Sat - in Doll. ___

She's no - bo - dy's fool, so I'm play - ing it cool as can be, ___

I'll give it a whirl, ___ but I

COME SUNDAY
from "Black, Brown and Beige"

Words & Music by Duke Ellington

TAKE THE "A" TRAIN

Words and Music by Billy Strayhorn